DAD JOKES

THE ULTIMATE COLLECTION
FOR THE FAMILY COMEDIAN

JIM CHUMLEY

summersdale

An Hachette UK Company
www.hachette.co.uk

Summersdale Publishers Ltd
Part of Octopus Publishing Group Limited
Carmelite House
50 Victoria Embankment
LONDON
EC4Y 0DZ
UK

www.summersdale.com

Printed and bound in the Czech Republic

ISBN: 978-1-78685-228-1

Substantial discounts on bulk quantities of Summersdale books are available to corporations, professional associations and other organisations. For details contact general enquiries: telephone: +44 (0) 1243 771107 or email: enquiries@summersdale.com.

TO..............................

FROM..........................

What time did the man go to the dentist?

Tooth hurt-y.

A ham sandwich walks into a bar and orders a beer. The bartender says, 'Sorry, we don't serve food here.'

5/4 of people admit
that they're bad
with fractions.

Two guys walk into
a bar, the third
one ducks.

Why do chicken coops
only have two doors?
Because if they had
four, they would be
chicken sedans.

**Why did the
man give the pony
a glass of water?**

Because he was
a little horse.

**What's brown
and sticky?**

A stick.

**How do you make
a tissue dance?**

Put a little boogie in it.

What was the name of the emperor penguin?

Julius Freezer.

Kid: Hey, I was thinking...

....

Dad: I thought I smelled something burning.

If you ever get cold just stand in a corner for a bit. They are usually around 90 degrees.

Did you hear about the restaurant on the moon? Great food, no atmosphere.

What's Forrest Gump's password?

1forrest1

What did one lawyer say to the other lawyer?

We are both lawyers.

**RIP boiled water.
You will be mist.**

**I'm reading a book
about anti-gravity.
It's impossible to
put down!**

Where did Napoleon keep his armies?

Up his sleevies.

What's white and can't climb trees?

A fridge.

I just watched a documentary about beavers. It was the best dam show I ever saw!

Have you ever tried eating a clock? It's very time-consuming.

Kid: Dad, did you
get a haircut?

Dad: No, I got
them all cut.

Want to hear a joke about a piece of paper? Never mind... it's tearable.

How do you approach an angry Welsh cheese?

Caerphilly.

And Jesus said,
'Come forth and
receive eternal life.'
But John came fifth,
and won a toaster.

Spring is here!
I got so excited
I wet my plants!

Do you want to hear a
word I just made up?

Plagiarism.

How many tickles does it take to make an octopus laugh?

Ten-tickles.

*Driving past
a graveyard*

**Dad: Do you know why
I can't be buried there?**

....

Kid: Why not?

....

**Dad: Because I'm
not dead yet!**

A friend of mine died recently after drinking a gallon of varnish. It was a horrible end, but a lovely finish.

What do you call a cow with two legs?

Lean beef.

What do you call a cow with no legs?

Ground beef.

I'm not addicted to brake fluid. I can stop whenever I want.

Did you hear about the man who stole a calendar? He got 12 months.

What's the best part
about living
in Switzerland?
I don't know, but the
flag is a big plus.

Why couldn't the bike stand up by itself?

It was two-tyred.

Today I gave away all
my dead batteries
free of charge.

I'm only familiar
with 25 letters in the
English language.
I don't know why.

**Kid: Dad, are you
all right?**

....

Dad: No, I'm half left.

**What did the 0
say to the 8?**

Nice belt.

**Why are skeletons
so calm?**

Nothing gets under
their skin.

Did you hear about
the circus fire?
It was in tents!

An invisible man
married an invisible
woman. The kids were
nothing to look
at either.

**Why do you
never see elephants
hiding in trees?**

Because they're
so good at it.

You heard of that new band 1023 MB? They're good but they haven't got a gig yet.

A man walks into a library and asks: 'Have you got any books on shelves?'

The rotation of
the earth really
makes my day.

Have you heard of the
music group called
Cellophane? They
mostly wrap.

Did you hear about the cheese factory that exploded in France? There was nothing left but de Brie.

What's blue and smells like red paint?

Blue paint.

The future, the present and the past walked into a bar. Things got a little tense.

Don't spell part backwards. It's a trap.

Mum: How do I look?

....

Dad: With your eyes.

Why did the can crusher quit his job?

Because it was soda-pressing.

What lies at the bottom of the ocean and twitches?

A nervous wreck.

I've just been diagnosed as colour-blind. I know, it certainly has come out of the purple.

I was interrogated over the theft of a cheese toastie. Man, they really grilled me.

Why didn't the toilet paper cross the road?

It got stuck in a crack.

How many apples grow on a tree?

All of them.

**Waiter: If you
need anything, my
name is Joe.**

....

**Dad: What if we don't
need anything?**

A magic tractor drives down the road and turns into a field.

I hate jokes about German sausages. They're the wurst.

Do you want to hear a joke about construction?

Nah, I'm still working on it.

Why did the baker have brown hands?

Because he
kneaded a poo.

Two peanuts were
walking down
the street.
One was a salted.

I don't trust stairs.
They're always up
to something.

**What do you call
a fake noodle?**

An impasta.

How did the hipster burn his tongue?

He drank his coffee before it was cool.

Kid: Dad, can you
put my shoes on?

....

Dad: I don't think
they'll fit me.

I used to have a job
at a calendar factory
but I got the sack
because I took a
couple of days off.

Have you heard the rumour going round about butter?

Never mind, I shouldn't spread it.

What did the pirate say when he turned 80?

Aye-matey.

A jump lead walks into a bar. The bartender says, 'I'll serve you, but don't start anything.'

I used to hate facial hair, but then it grew on me.

**Why did the
stadium get hot
after the game?**

All of the fans left.

What did the duck say to the bartender?

Put it on my bill.

I have a few jokes about unemployed people but it doesn't matter. None of them work.

How did Ebenezer Scrooge win the football game?

The ghost of Christmas passed.

What's ET short for?

Because he's only got little legs!

**What do you call
500 penguins in
Trafalgar Square?**

Lost.

I went to a seafood
disco last week...
I pulled a mussel.

I'd tell you a chemistry
joke but all the good
ones argon.

What's the difference between a good joke and a bad joke timing.

What do you call cheese that's not yours?

Nacho cheese.

Don't trust atoms.
They make up
everything!

I went to buy some
camouflage trousers
the other day, but I
couldn't find any.

What kind of fish is made of only two sodium atoms?

2 Na.

Why did the bull win an award?

Because he was outstanding in his field.

I went to the corner shop today. I bought four corners.

I'd like to give a big shout-out to pavements for keeping me off the streets.

Why can't you have a nose 12 inches long?

Because then it would be a foot.

I went on a
once-in-a-lifetime
holiday. Never again.

A Buddhist walks up
to a hotdog stand and
says, 'Make me one
with everything.'

Why does a flamingo stand on one leg?

If it didn't stand on any it'd fall over.

**Cashier: Would you
like the milk
in a bag, sir?**

....

**Dad: No, just leave it
in the carton.**

Our wedding was so beautiful, even the cake was in tiers.

A termite walks into a bar and says, 'Where is the bar tender?'

What's the difference between an African elephant and an Indian elephant?

About 5,000 miles.

What does an angry pepper do?

It gets
jalapeño face.

Kid: Dad, what's your best joke?

....

Dad: You.

Some people say they
pick their nose but
I feel like I was just
born with mine.

I really understand
how batteries feel
because I'm rarely
included in
things either.

**Why can't you hear
a pterodactyl go to
the bathroom?**

Because the
pee is silent.

How do you make a sausage roll?

Put it on top of a hill and push it.

Kid: Dad, can I
watch TV?

....

Dad: Yes, but don't
turn it on.

You kill vegetarian
vampires with a steak
to the heart.

I used to be a banker
but I lost interest.

Why couldn't the lifeguard save the hippy?

He was too far out, man!

What's red and bad
for your teeth?

A brick.

Did you hear about the Mexican train killer? He had locomotives.

Time flies like an arrow but fruit flies like a banana.

Why was the sand embarrassed?

Because the seaweed.

How do you make holy water?

You boil the hell out of it.

**Kid: Dad, can you
make me a sandwich?**

....

**Dad: Poof, you're
a sandwich!**

Did you hear about those new corduroy pillows? They're making headlines everywhere!

My friend recently got crushed by a pile of books, but he's only got his shelf to blame.

Guess why I like jokes about lifts?

They work on so many levels.

Why was the baby strawberry crying?

Because his mum and dad were in a jam.

I'm glad I know
sign language. It's
pretty handy.

Last night I went
to a comedy and
philosophy convention.
Laughed more than
I thought.

What do you call a factory that sells passable products?

A satisfactory.

What do you call a man who likes cheese?

A man who likes cheese.

Dad: My mate's
working in a
bowling alley.

....

Kid: Ten pin?

....

Dad: No, permanent.

eBay is useless. I tried to look up lighters, but all they had was 13,839 matches.

I just ate a frozen apple. Hardcore.

Why did the invisible man turn down the job offer?

He couldn't see himself doing it.

**How does a penguin
build his house?**

Igloos it together.

I'm terrified of lifts.
I'm going to start
taking steps to
avoid them.

I slept like a log last
night. I woke up in
the fireplace.

**Kid: Dad, what
time is it?**

....

**Dad: I don't know, it
keeps changing.**

What do you call
a deer with no eyes?

No idea!

What do you call a deer with no legs and no eyes?

Still no idea!

What do you call a deer with no legs and no eyes when you throw it in a swimming pool?

Bob!

A red and a blue
ship collided in the
Caribbean. Apparently
the survivors were
marooned.

I bought a dog from
my local blacksmith.
When I got it home
it made a bolt
for the door.

**How do you organise
a party in space?**

You planet.

Last night my wife and I watched three movies back to back.
Luckily, I was the one facing the TV.

A courtroom artist was arrested today for an unknown reason... the details are sketchy.

What does a house wear?

A dress.

What do you call a bagel that can fly?

A plain bagel.

I was trying to explain puns to my kleptomaniac friend today, but she kept taking things literally.

I stole a rabbit today. Then I had to make a run for it.

Dad: What's the difference
between a piano, a tuna
and a pot of glue?

Kid: I don't know.

Dad: You can tuna piano,
but you can't piano a tuna!

Kid: What about the glue?

Dad: I knew you'd get stuck there.

What does a time traveller do when he's hungry?

He goes back four seconds.

What do you call a fat psychic?

A four-chin teller.

Someone stole my mood ring. I don't know how I feel about that.

My grandad has the heart of a lion and a lifetime ban from the zoo.

Kid: Why are you staring at the orange juice?

....

Dad: It says concentrate.

Why did the picture go to jail?

It was framed.

What did the digital clock say to the grandfather clock?

Look, grandpa, no hands!

A plateau is the highest form of flattery.

A woman told me she recognised me from the vegetarian club, but I'd never met herbivore.

What do lawyers wear to court?

Lawsuits.

What do you get when you cross a snowman with a vampire?

Frostbite.

I wouldn't buy
anything with Velcro.
It's a total rip-off.

Just watched a
documentary on
how ships are kept
together. Riveting.

Son: Dad, can you pass me my sunglasses?

....

Dad: Only if you can pass me my dadglasses.

**What did the red light
say to the green light?**

Don't look,
I'm changing!

What did the policeman say to his belly button?

You are under a vest.

My wife told me I was
a fool to build a car
out of spaghetti.
You should have seen
the look on her face
when I drove pasta.

Kid: I'll call you later.

....

Dad: Please don't do that. I've always asked you to call me Dad!

What do you call a fish with no eyes?

A fsh.

What's the loudest
pet you can get?
A trumpet.

I told my friend she
drew her eyebrows
too high. She seemed
surprised.

Nostalgia isn't what
it used to be.

What did the buffalo say to his son when he dropped him off at school?

Bison.

A farmer counted 196 cows in his field, but when he rounded them up he had 200.

Jokes about opticians just get cornea and cornea.

Why don't skeletons go trick-or-treating?

Because they have no body to go with.

Kid: Hold on, I think I've got something in my shoe.

....

Dad: Is it your foot?

Life without geometry is pointless.

Did you hear about the kidnapping at school? It's fine, he woke up.

What do you call bears with no ears?

B.

**What did the grape
do when he got
stepped on?**

He let out a little wine.

**Bought a litre
of correction
fluid yesterday.
Huge mistake.**

**I've started a business
building yachts in my
attic. Sails are going
through the roof.**

What did one snowman say to the other?

'Do you smell carrots?'

**Why did the squid
go into battle?**

He was well-armed.

I stayed up all
night to see where
the sun went. Then it
dawned on me.

Two satellites decided
to get married. The
wedding wasn't much
but the reception
was incredible.

**Kid: Dad, what's
the time?**

....

**Dad: Time you got
a watch.**

A woman is on trial for burning her husband's guitar collection. Judge says, 'First offender?' She says, 'No, first a Gibson! Then a Fender!'

When does Friday come before Thursday?

In the dictionary.

I wondered why the frisbee was getting bigger. Then it hit me.

A steak pun is a rare medium well done.

Why is Peter Pan always flying?

He Neverlands.

**Why did the cookie
go to the hospital?**

Because it was feeling
a little crumby.

When you get a
bladder infection,
urine trouble.

I wrote a song
about a tortilla.
Well, actually, it's
more of a wrap.

**What do you call
a man with no nose
and no body?**

Nobody nose.

I was walking the dogs the other day when all of a sudden they vanished into thin air. Not sure where they went, but I've got some leads.

**Kid: Hey, Dad,
what's up?**

·····································

Dad: The ceiling.

Did you hear about the race between the lettuce and the tomato?

The lettuce was a head and the tomato was trying to ketchup.

Sometimes I tuck my knees to my chest and lean forward. That's just how I roll.

If you want a job in the moisturiser industry, the best advice I can give is to apply daily.

What do you call a belt
made out of watches?

A waist of time.

Shout out to the people who want to know what the opposite of in is.

I told my doctor that I broke my arm in two places. He told me to stop going to those places.

Kid: Dad, I'm hungry.

....

**Dad: Hello, Hungry,
I'm dad!**

If you're interested in
finding out more about
our books, find us on Facebook at
Summersdale Publishers and follow
us on Twitter at **@Summersdale**.

www.summersdale.com

Image credits